# A

# WALK

# IN

# THE

# SKIES

TROY HARMON

Fulton Books
Meadville, PA

Published by Fulton Books 2024

ISBN 979-8-89221-907-5 (paperback)
ISBN 979-8-89221-908-2 (digital)

Printed in the United States of America

I'd like to dedicate this book to
my mom, Judy Hamilton.
May she fly with angels.
Rest in peace, Mom.

With special thanks to the following:
Amy Hamilton
Matthew Williams
Brock Vernon for taking my photo
All my family and friends

# INFINITE ROADS

I will travel these infinite roads we call life,
I will fight death 'til the end of my time,
And hope I will be welcomed on the other side.

*Thank you.*
*Hope you enjoy the book*

Troy Harmon

## Into a Starlit Sky

On the wings of angels I fly,
Deep into a starlit sky,
Soaring Orion's Belt and past the Milky Way,
Watching as Earth faded away,
I thought of home.

## Born to Say Goodbye

As the days get cooler,
As the days get shorter,
As the evenings get longer,
I hear the road calling, Travelin' Man,
I think I was born to say goodbye,
But then again,
Weren't we all?

## Seasons of the Mind

If you decided not to go,
If you talk yourself out of going,
You may have thought your way
Out of paradise.

## Legend

As I died,
The devil watched.
The devil grasped me
With all his might and said
I have taken darker souls to hell
But a warrior, a legend,
I will let pass.

## Wisdom

With the wisdom of many,
I create words, good and bad,
Seeing life from my eyes,
Deep within my mind,
If you look and follow slowly,
You will see
Your life and mine.

## For All That Follow

Out of life
I will go into death's hands,
I will travel
With no wisdom or visions

Of what's ahead or in store for me.
I will pray a prayer
For my family
And their future
And all that follow me.

## From the Alpha to the Omega

In the mist,
In the middle of it all,
You see yourself looking back,
Somewhere between regret and happiness.

## Pleasure and Pain

After we have lived,
After we have learned happiness and pain,
Fear not for we were brought on this earth
To experience pleasure and pain,
The gifts that were given to us.

## Souls of the Sunrise

Souls of the sunrise,
Symphonies of sundown,
The night's stars spin around and around,

Angels smile and demons frown,
And the moon stares at the earth
As it goes around and around
To get a glance at the phantoms of twilight
Outlined in black and white
As the souls of the sun rise again.

## Somewhere Between Life and Death

As long as there is a sunrise,
And a sunset,
And a twilight,
And a midnight,
A life and a death,
Dark and light,
There will always be
Poems to write.

## Diamond Eyes

Rainbows and gold,
Mountains and springs,
Thunder and lightning,
Iron and steel,
The skies with diamond eyes.

## Evening Dusk

People settling into the twilight
Quietly drifting into the night
Hazily hoping for salvation of the dawn.

## Into the Wild Blue

Pastures where dreams are born
And where eagles soar,
Where trees grow towards the sun,
And rain storms roar,
And streams grow into rivers
As the waterfalls pour
Into the wild blue.

## Ghosts of Midnight

A haunted poet of the highway
He writes seeing the world
From a warm summer sunrise
Into the evening
When the roads are cool,
Lonely ghosts of the midnight
Won't leave him alone,
Again he awakes
Again he writes.

## In the Background

God is the sunrise,
God is the sunset,
God is the stars and moon at midnight,
God is always around us,
God is in the background
Sometimes you have to stop and look to see.

## Between Here and There

In the great sadness,
I only hope that there is great happiness,
Somewhere between here and there.

## The Love

I think male or female,
Animal or human,
A universal feeling,
A thought, an instinct to protect,
Infinitely,
To live or to die
To protect
What we love.
Amen

## Through the Good and the Bad Times

Looking back
Home was either way we went
Somehow through the good times
And the bad times
The earth was turning
The days kept coming
And life went on.

## Live Like There's No Tomorrow

To live every day
Like there is no tomorrow,
To look into the eyes of Death,
To die looking Death in the eyes,
To smile into the eyes of Death
Is to have lived.

## You and I

Nothing will ever be right
But with a little help and happiness
I know everything will be alright.

## Peace of Mind

Wondering through my thoughts in darkness,
Finding that sleep is hard to find,
Lost so much,
Hoping that my dreams
Will give me peace of mind.

## What the Future Holds

The wind blew wicked through the land
As the righteous slept through the night,
The wild, the young, and the old
Prayed to their God or Gods
That the world from which they came
And from which they went
Would be free of war, hate, and greed
And to prepare the young, the old, and the wild
For what the future holds.

## To Live is Bravery, To Die is Easy

Into a universe,
Into a parallel,
Between time and space
I wander somewhere

Between the old and the new
Somewhere between the beginning and the end
Is where we are
Racing towards death like it's a finish line.

## In the Life

In the life that I want to live,
I got lost not knowing which way to go,
At the crossroads, I stopped and looked to the skies
And prayed to the good Lord, by 'n' by.

## Listen

I heard this person is going places,
And I heard you'll never go anywhere,
Someone once told me
If you never go You'll never know
So I quit looking back.

*For Vern*
*I was listening*

## In the Evening

They were always there
Now they're gone
I find myself in the evening
Wanting to call out to them.
Through the hard times
And the good times
They were always there
Sitting and talking and watching
The sun go down.

## As I Drift Back in Time

With remembering and dreams,
I drift back in time
To days when family and friends are still alive
In my memories and my dreams
They survive with this thought in mind,
As I drift back in time.

## War

As the twilight fades into darkness,
The human race prepares for war.

## Fading Darkness

In fading darkness
The evening falls across the land
With winter whispering in our ears
As the sun faded away
The stars and the moon shined bright
Again was born another day.

## Into the Gray-Silver Sunset

Slowly and as slow as I can go,
Into the gray-silver sunset I go,
You can never be prepared
For the age and the wisdom
Of the days of old,
Into the gray-silver sunset I go.

## The Question

As the wheels start to run,
And the wind begins to blow,
And the sounds of the unknown begin to play,
I get a feeling inside that asks a question,
Will I make it back home?
And I pray.

## Nowhere

In the dark corners of our mind,
There is freedom.
Your hopes, your dreams,
And you will find me there.

## Knowledge and Wisdom

As the sun begins to rise
The past becomes the future
As fast as the speed of light
As we learn more and more about ourselves
And the universe we live in.
Our knowledge becomes our wisdom
As fast as the future becomes the past
With this poem being said, wrote, or read,
Aren't we all the same in our soul?

## Down the Road

As I walk down the road,
Into the evening
Then into the dark
The shadows of my mind
Begin to haunt me
Of friends and family I've lost along the road.

## Without Meaning

There has to be a meaning
Without meaning or an idea or a dream
Without them, there is nothing.

## Paved in Gold

As I drive down this infinite road
Some say the road is lost,
Some say the road is paved in gold.
Heaven or hell,
Either way I go,
The stories will be told.

## The Call

Living so fast,
We take for granted, life,
Who said that?
He said that.
No, she said that.
When you get that call
When life gets shorter.

# The Answer

I think in life
That a person should do their part
Not ignore what's in their heart
What they think is right
We enter this world once
And we leave it once,
If I go before my maker
When asked I want to have an answer.

*I gave it my best.*

# The Winds

A loving blue sky,
With the sun up so high,
With trees swaying
And chimes singing,
And the earth turning,
Along with our lives
Ever changing like the winds.

## The Saint

When the essence of life is discovered
Sins will not be as we think, they will be
As we believe the saint.

## On a Somber Sunday Morning

With an eerie ebony dawn,
On a somber Sunday morning,
The earth slowly turning
With the early morning mists
Floating gently above the fields
I think of the past,
As the present drifts in the wind,
I awake to a world
I once knew.
Amen.

## Our Future

Children haven't a choice in our quest,
Teach them, love them,
And our future shall be bright.

## Slumber and Sunrise

In the midnight,
Somewhere between
Slumber and sunrise,
A voice whispered to me,
Somewhere between
Night and day
It said everything
Is going to be okay.

## Love, Hate, and Fear

Life and dreams parallel the mind,
Is one with the body,
Stars upon stars, visions upon visions,
Beyond the mountains, beyond the seas,
The universe far as the eye can see,
If you listen you can hear humanities,
Love, hate, and fear.

## Standing on the Mountain

And the land filled with darkness
As I stood on the mountain
Watching the stars light

And I felt alone
As the dusk faded into night
I dream, of dreams
Of heaven into the sweet by and by.
Amen.

## Standing in the Valley

And the land filled with light
As we stood in the valley
Watching the stars fading,
We seemed alone
As the moon faded into fire
We dream, of dreams
Of heaven in the sweet by and by.

## Adrift

Being lost in an ocean
Of thought and emotion,
Adrift in a universe
That is not our own can be
And is no place for any human being,
Stand up, take control,
It is your choice.

## Decisions of Life

When the things we love come true,
Our dreams, our thoughts, our humanity,
Hoping we make the decisions of our future,
Make them be the right ones.

## Listen

Listening to the night
Listening to the day
Listen as the symphonies of life play.

## Eyes of Mama

Looking into the eyes of Mama
She taught me to love,
But not to be a fool.
Death awaits us all,
Rich, poor, good, or evil
Like an early morning sunrise
Or a warm summer sunset
Like the day and the night
Our life will end.

## Dancing on Clouds

Into the deepest night we float,
As we think good thoughts of tomorrow,
Dancing on clouds and looking for silver linings,
I dream of castles and pearly gates,
A place called heaven
Where friends and family await.

## Silver Moon

Silver moon full of glow
With powers beyond our control,
See us through the darkness and the unknown,
The brighter you shine,
The more mysterious you become.
God only knows,
What we would do without your glow.

## Last of My Breed

I am the last of my breed,
There will never be another like me,
Nor will there ever be,
Within these words I say
Somewhere between night and day,

I am the last of my breed,
There will be no one
Before or after me on the earth
I was born to the earth
I will return,
Ashes to ashes,
Dust to dust.

## February Sky

On a cool February morning,
The sun came up on a mysterious dawn,
The human race and the wind, the sun,
And the moon, and the stars,
And the blue skies see the outline
Of heaven in the eyes of a crisp February sunrise.

## American Pride Forever

Freedom of choice and to choose on any level
Should be sacred and should be protected,
Every man,
Every woman,
Every child,
Every race,
Every religion.

## Spirits of Fire

Into the heavens
With angels dancing
Across the skies,
Into the evenings
With dark angels
Whispering lullabies,
Through the midnight
Softly, the winds cry
As the spirits of fire
Begin to arise.

## To Protect From Evil

Freedom choice clothe our poor,
Feed our children,
Strong people of God,
We do what's in our soul to do,
To protect from evil.

## It Was a Beautiful Day Today

It was a beautiful day today,
Where were you at the end of the world?
Singing, dancing, loving, celebrating,

Sleeping, dreaming,
Or listening to the echoes
Of the end dancing across the wind,
Partaking in the spirits of what a beautiful day.
Amen

## Peace, Love, and Salvation

Men, women, and children, fathers, sons
And daughters scream to the heavens for
Peace, love, and salvation for our existence.

## Mother's Eyes

Life is a stream
Pouring down a mountainside,
Light and warmth
Bring life to the world,
After the storms subside,
The stars appear,
Love remains,
A mother gives strength and warmth
Under her eyes.

*Love,*
*Troy*

## Forever and Again

Have you ever watched the sunset
The beautiful flash
Just before it hides it's head
It is like the sun is saying goodnight,
I'll see you tomorrow
And forever
And again
And again.

## Praying for Tomorrow

Knowing that pieces of me vanish
When family and friends pass into the heavens
Makes me wonder if there will be anything
Left of me here or after.

## Ever and Ever

Pink flower into shades of jade
Powers of the mind make the soul
Infinite in life and in death.

# The Glimmering Light

Satanic symphonies
Play through the night,
Demons sing
And angels hide,
Angels waiting
For one glimmering light
That breaks through
Destroying the demons
One by two.

# Hover World

Hovering worlds
Above the clouds,
Soaring above
Their thoughts and dreams,
Stories, songs, and lullabies
Are created from impossible dreams
Becoming reality,
Our dreams come true.

## Psychedelic Symphonies

Psychedelic flowers amongst the fields,
A growth of a zillion dreams,
The earth weaving
The psychedelic seeds.

## Peace Forever

When the war came to an end,
Love, peace, and salvation,
Reign free across the human race,
In conclusion, I am a child of peace.

## Unchained Beauty

Free as the warm summer winds,
An outlaw beauty
Crossing the border into freedom,
A wild, enchanted dark angel
Riding a Midwestern tornado into eternity.

## A Dark Beauty

As the sun went down,
I thought
Hope
Dreams
Fading light
Turning to darkness,
A different beauty,
A dark beauty
Where hopes and dreams
Still exist.

## The Slowly Dusk

As demons slowly invade my mind,
I search the world for angels
That will defend the salvation of my soul.

## Our Land

The stars and the heavens are glowing,
I know that every day I awake,
The sun is shining somewhere
On our sacred land
That feeds us, clothes us, shelters us from ourselves.

## The Wizard Awoke

The wizard awoke from a thousand-year sleep.
The wind rose high into the heavens,
Bright into the night
The moon smiled at the sun.
The dark smiled at the light, for a moment,
Into twilight and beyond there was peace.

## Lonely Nights

Sometimes I feel the lonesome nights
Sometimes I feel them drifting in,
Sometimes I just smile
And let them lonesome nights
Drift on by.

## Looking Into Myself

As I look into myself,
I feel sometimes in my life
I haven't been as good of a person
That I always wanted to be.
Out of ignorance unknown
Out of pain maybe
But I am only human
And who I am now.

## In Life and In Death

I'll be watching in my death
Keeping an eye on you,
I'll be there in spirit if you go wrong
I'll be there to guard you from evil
I'll be there.

## Laughing, Singing, and Dancing

I can just see them in the light
Laughing, singing, and dancing
In the morning or in the moonlight
Or at night with the rain pouring,
Laughing, singing, and dancing,
We'll be there to meet you when it's time
Laughing, singing, and dancing.

## Western Skies

A flash in the western skies
Into the darkest night
Into the soaring skies approaching
Where the moonlight meets the fire.

## Highways

Your dreams await you
Down the highways and byways of life,
I was always better at hello than goodbye,
It's never goodbye,
It's just I'll see you down the highway.

## To Say Hello

The deeper you feel,
The harder you cry,
It's always better to say hello
Than it is to say goodbye,
With this being said,
I say hello
And not goodbye.

## Enjoy It

Everything has an end,
Me, you, the trees,
Grass, the heavens, and the earth,
So enjoy life, celebrate it,
Enjoy it, don't destroy it.

## Friendship

Every second is a new day,
Every minute is a new friend,
With every friendship, there's a bond,
Every day has a night,
Every night has a day,
Where there is friendship, love, and family,
There is a way.

## Looking Back

Pain, love, lust, and fear,
I miss the days when I was there,
As I look back,
Maybe I really wasn't there at all,
Least not the kid, boy, young man
That I knew or know now.

## Every Day Is a New Day

In hard times, in bad times,
The soul, the will of a human being
Is at its highest
Look ahead, look behind, take a deep breath
Out and in and out again,

Begin your trip over again
Every day, every night, morning, and twilight,
A new life is always ahead.

## A Child's Eyes

In a child's eyes, dreams come true,
Every day is a sunrise,
The stars and the moon shine,
The future smiles at a child's eyes.

## Midnight Memories

Ashes still remain
Where a faint ghost you can still see
In the midnight memories of your mind
Forever remembered
Never forgotten Fox Farm.

## A Piece in a Puzzle

Death is a piece in the puzzle
That I can't overcome
Every time something I love fades
Into memory
It shakes the pillars of my heart.

## Crazy Daze

In a crazy world,
The world seems very crazy,
You may have to be a little crazy
Just to survive some of them, crazy daze.

## Unforgotten Sky

Into the abyss death rising high
To the far side of good
By standing tall between the darkness
Of unforgotten sky
The deeper we fly the higher we climb.

## The Road to Eternity

I will never give up
I will never die
I am forever on the road to eternity.

## RIP

The spirits soar into the glow of the heavens
Stars shine dim on a pale and glowing field
Of rest and respect and love forever yours.

## Into the Unknown

A sunset with streams and valleys not knowing
What's ahead or what the dawn brings
Or the sun rising into a new day,
Maybe the mysteries of heaven and earth,
Make the not knowing, worth living.

## Without Compassion

The powers that be
Tell you what they want you to hear
Only let you be what they want you to be
Humanity will destroy their self
Without compassion
There will be no tomorrow.

## Into the Depths

I've walked into the halls of death
I've driven down the eternal road
Flown high with the angels
Looked down into hell
I do not fear what I have done
I only fear what I will do.

## The Afterlife

Do not fear change for life is an adventure
Each day and night is a crusade
For glory, fame, and riches
For it is not over
Till your family greets you in the afterlife.

## Twilight and Fire

Echoes of oblivion soar through the sky
Night turns into day and day turns into night.
The moon is red with traces of black
And white psychedelic storm
Is in the mist of a morning
Of twilight and of fire,
And we dream of oblivion.

## Infinity

Lost and gone into infinity
Some of my favorite dreams,
Some of the best of myself can be found
Lost and gone into infinity
If you find that dream, you'll find me
Lost and gone into infinity.

## To a Lost and Found Friend

I'll see you around friend
The days have ended for you
Troubled and lonesome are over and done
Going to see Mamma and Dad
I'll see you around friend.

## Live and Love Life

Even though our life and our decisions
Are wrong or right
I think as long as we live and love life
We will live and love life
In the before and afterlife.

## Shadows of Twilight

A pale moon on a dark starlit night
A war-axed warrior stands
With demons in the shadows of twilight
Waiting for his next battle.

## Wind Dancer

To Cousin James,
Wind dancing across electric skies
Lightning strikes bright
Chasing all shadows away.
Love Troy

## Into the Heavens

No thought of living or dying did we fill
Hate had left our souls
Happiness was born into our life
Memories are all we have
When we pass into the heavens.

## Destination Unknown

Heaven and hell, good and bad
The very things that make us exist
Can destroy us or enjoy us.
Living is hard to prepare for
As to death is to be at peace.

## Never Forgotten

When the wind blows,
Echoes of the lost are never forgotten
In life there is darkness, within death,
There is beauty beyond our imagination.
Amen

## The Vow

A warrior among warriors
A warrior of God
A warrior of peace
A dreamer of dreams
A warrior of men.

## Fountain

As life passes by
The mind must occupy
When staring into the abyss
Eternity is at your doorstep.

## It's Better

It's better to have lived this life I've lived
On this earth, good and bad
I always have said and always will
I wouldn't have missed it for the world.

## The Soul

In vengeance there is death
In death there is life
In spirit there is soul
In soul there is eternal wisdom
In what is, what was, and what will be.

## Day and Night

The universe of black and gray
Stars spinning into the Milky Way,
A silver moon spinning around the earth,
Turning day to night and night to day.

## A Different Life

I slowly awoke to the sounds of hope
Strange dreams of the future
Seeing children grow up
Seeing a different life
Not better not worse
Just a different life.

## The Quest

Into the dark
Not knowing where the dark will end
And the light will begin
Not afraid of that lonesome quest
The night has in store
Into the sands of time we pour.

## Of the Reaping

When the hand of God
Reaches out for me
I will reach out and take it
For a warrior's path is of peace
I will not fear death
I will call Him friend.

## Realms of Lust

In the pits of the unknown
Thoughts and feelings do not exist
To care does not exist
In the realms of lust.

## The World Believed

It's like I can see back to the beginning of time
When the human race was resurrected
And our sins were left behind
And the world believed
And was resurrected into the light.

## Colors of Your Eyes

Hiding your secrets in the
Darkness of your mind is sometimes
Better than wearing your secrets
In the colors of your eyes.

## The Answer

Looking for the answer
Just a sign to let me know
That everybody is going to be alright.

## Eternal Skies

As I walked out of the valley,
Of the shadow of death
I stood on the mountain
And saw the last unicorn
Grazing in the green pastures.
I saw the tree of life as I passed by.
I saw the serpent curled up in the tree of temptation
I saw the predator lying with prey
As angels sang beautiful
Into the vast eternal skies.

## Lullabies of Heaven

Into Heaven with a whisper,
Out of this life with just a glimmer,
A place in darkness where there is light,
An echo in the wind,
Angels singing
Lullabies of heaven.

# Blink of an Eye

In the times that we live in, it seems that we are waiting, listening, watching very carefully, studying the world around us, waiting for that special moment when we will start enjoying life. That moment, is now, always, and forever. Now, I think sometimes, the world needs to be told, or reminded, that this second, this minute, this moment, is that time, your time, to live and enjoy life in a nonbeat of a heart. Your world could be changed forever in the blink of an eye. So enjoy life the seconds the minutes, the moments, of your life from this point on. Don't wish your time away because time is short.

# Lonesome and Wandering

The winds whistling across the land, with the
Storms drifting in, the skies blue and pale white,
The highs today, that would be three, flying
Bright, lonesome, and wandering, stories being told,
    wondering about tomorrow, hoping that tomorrow is better than today, always, amen. With happiness and grief, I say to you, we only go around once on earth, so don't waste it.

## Old Soul

Just an old soul, drifting far into the mountains,
Drifting by, like clouds, on a cold winter's day,
Gray-silver highlights in the sunset, passing by like
The sunrise, rivers rolling through the valleys,
Winding its way across, our country, that we call
    home, searching for one destination the
    almighty ocean, just to call that place home.

## I Will Run No More

A demon, a dark form, that haunts you in your dreams,
    that you've been running from for a very long
    time, it tires you, and one day you wake up,
And say to yourself, I will run no more,
The dream the nightmare is just a day away, so you
    lay your head down to sleep. And the dark form
    is after you again. You turn to the beast and say
    no more. The beast stops. You sense fear in his
    eyes. I am not afraid of you. I will run no more.
    Then the beast turns, flees back to hell from
    which it came. Demons are bullies; if you stand
    up to them, they will run away. They feed on
    your fears. They are cowards. Send them back
    to hell where they belong.

## Where I Go When I Dream

I am on the battlefields, in battle, against evil,
I am climbing, the greatest mountains,
I am standing before the raging, mitty, rising ocean,
I am traveling the universe, at light speed, among,
The stars and planets, in search of new life forms,
I travel time, saving humanity, fighting wars, against
    demons, for which you cannot see,
That's where I go when I sleep.

## Wisdom of the Past

With the wisdom of the past, I prepare, myself,
For what's ahead or what's up the road, I've been
    down the road of life, stories that have been told
    of my life, good and bad, I will go on living my
    life, standing for what I think is right. I may
    not start the fight, but I will finish it; with that
    being said, I will finish this life to the end.

## Think of Me

Think of me on a Sunday
Just before the sunrise, when
You're laughing with your best friends,

When you're listening to your
Favorite songs, and when the ocean rises
And falls, think of me when the mist
Is rising from a lake on a cool summer's day,
When kids are playing, in the quiet of your mind.
Knowing that it's okay, think of me.

## Peace, Honor, and Bravery

Our lives as we get older, sometimes it seems like
only the strong survive, so we survive our lives,
Till we meet, Grim the Reaper, and we meet our
maker, looking back on my life as I look forward to the future. I do not worry or fear death
or meeting my maker; what troubles my mind
from time to time is my life. In the eyes of the
ones I love and the ones that love and look up to
me. This is the thought that troubles me. With
in this poem, I pray I am only human, flesh and
blood, and it is God's will that I pass this way,
peace, honor, and bravery. Amen. 🙏

# Question

Out of the past into the future, family, growing up
Family growing old,
As days years go by,
I look into the night skies, to only be glad that I did.
I don't know what is out there or beyond our life,
The energy of life escaping into infinity. Blood and
bone going back into the earth from which it
was created. The alpha or the omega, that's the
Question. Or could it be both?
The Big Show
I keep a watchful eye on death,
For no one knows what, death is,
Is it the end or the beginning,
Of something bigger than us,
Larger than life, if you will, maybe
Life is a practice run, a simulation, a
Rehearsal, for what I have come to know as the big
show.

## Young and Strong

In the late hours, when I am alone and my world
Is quiet and resting, I get lost in my thoughts
Of my family and friends and all the good times, the
sad times we all had, we stood tall and proud as
we were in our youth, as young and as strong as
we would ever be again. I know, as I fall into a
sleep, that I would do it all again Amen.

## Journey of Life

On this journey of life, it is the journey
Not the destination, that matters, for it is the most
important journey, we will ever take, we can
find, love, happiness, sorrow, knowledge, and
wisdom. Along the way, we can give back, to this
world some of what we've taken, the warmth of
a summer's day, the coolness of a summer's evening, to have made a difference in one person's
world with a word and a smile.

## Happy New Year

With the end so near, as the years are changing,
Days turn to evenings, midnights turn to mornings,
As reality becomes dreams, sunshine becomes the
      clouds, the rain becomes tears, as another year
      has
Disappeared; with this I say, "Happy New Year."

## Don't Live Too Fast

In to the winds, with the stars shining bright,
The storms have risen, and the storms have subsided,
And my life moving forward and not backward with
      heavens angels singing, go forward and spread
      the word with demons around every curve, I say
      to myself keep,
One eye on the road and the other on the rearview,
      for every story has a beginning like every story
      has an end.

## Within My Dreams

Every night when I sleep, I travel across, space and time, into the future, into the past, above and below and beyond. Dreams, as I am traveling these worlds within my dreams, across millennium after millennium, I encounter happiness and sorrow from which I can almost remember but just all fading into soft lullabies and sad melodies and joyous songs. Amen.

## Gentle into the Eve

With so many lives going out with
A bang, with my life day by day,
With the earth moving slow and even
Slowly, with death not knocking but
Around every corner, gentle into the eve
I go, looking forward and not looking back,
It's always the now, it's always the today and never
the past. Amen.

## The Definition of a Man

I think the definition of a man,
Is that you can't and will never stop walking
Down enough roads, enough highways,
        climb enough mountains,
I believe that a man will eternally
Search through his life and his thoughts.
That he could be the best man, he possibly could be.
Time for change
Every day is a good day,
To start again, every, second,
There's always time for change,
There's always time to change your ways. Amen.

## From Another Time

Into the future I go, faster than the speed of light.
Twenty-some years have passed in the blink of an
eye, just seeing the sights, smelling the roses one
more time, just passing through, just a visitor from
another time.

## We, the Human Race and All of Humanity

We, the human race
Stand isolated but not alone; hope comforts us, hope
      for our family, hope for our friends, hope for
      our future, love compassion in a time of sorrow,
What does not destroy us will only bring us together
      and only make us stronger.

## A Good Day to Die

In the time of gods,
A warrior's honor was to die
A brave, fearless, death
In, my time of death,
I only hope that I die,
An honorable, fearless,
Death in the eyes
Of God.

## Spirits of Fire

Into the heavens with angels dancing across the skies,
into the evenings with dark angels whispering lullabies, through the midnight softly the winds cry, as
the spirits of fire begin to arise.

## Ghosts of Midnight

A haunted poet of the highway, he writes, seeing the world from a warm summer sunrise, into the hot highway, into the evening when the winds are cool, lonely ghosts of midnight won't leave him alone, again he awakens, again he writes.

## As I Drift Back in Time

With remembering and dreams, I drift back in time to days when family and friends are still alive; in my memories and in my dreams, they survive with this thought in mind as I drift back in time.

## Wish Young and Wish Well

I guess in this life, our thoughts, our feelings, and our lives do not turn out the way we wanted them to. Wish young and wish well, and maybe, just maybe, it all will come true.

## Into Eternity

The other side is never far away,
But only as far as you want it to be, steady as you go,
    into Eternity.

## Skies of Fire

The Pegasus, soaring high
Into the night sky, Slowly descending, into the abyss,
    of our minds.

## Infinite Roads

I will travel these infinite roads we call
Life, I will fight death till the end of my
Time, and I hope I will be welcomed on
The other side.

## Into the Night

Into the night, I drift
The darkness has no end,
There is a strange comfort in the
Night, as dreams fill the air, faint
Lullabies of peace, come from within,
Into the darkness, I descend.

## Phantoms Midnight

Darkness falls across a cool crimson sky, a full moon
comes up on a shaded timeless evening, the
winds rise from the valleys and cool a phantoms
midnight.
Standing on the mountain
And the land filled with darkness,
As I stood on the mountain,
Watching the star's fading light,
And I felt alone, as the dusk faded
Into night. I dreamt of dreams of
Heaven, into the sweet by and by.

## End of the Road

When the trail you're on has no end,
When the path you're on seems to never end, just
remember,
every road, every path, every trail,
Has an end,
Live every second of every minute,
Of every day.

## Twinkling of an Eye

In the night, a blue summer twilight,
With storms, not very far away, I dream
Back when things were simple, the stars were stars,
  the moon was the moon, and every day went by
  like a twinkling of an eye. With this I say I look
  forward to every new day, a new dawn, to a new
  dusk, and eternity will smile at your life.

## The Poem

In the night, a blue summer twilight,
With storms, not very far away, I dream
Back when things were simple, the stars were stars,
  the moon, was the moon and every day went by
  like a twinkling of an eye. With this I say I look
  forward to every new day, a new dawn, to a new
  dusk, and eternity will smile at your life.

## The Mighty Ocean

I had something it wanted. It must have spotted it
  the first time we met. So mighty, it always gets
  what it wants. It waited its moment and swept
  my treasure from my neck.

## Surprise Me

I don't want to be ready for my death,
I've heard when it's your time, well...
It's your time. My idea of being ready for death, well,
    I don't want; so surprise me.

## Darkened Was the Night

Rising into the night, darkened as the night so bright,
    seeing twilight as I am drifting into a dream,
    then out again, not knowing where the dream
    starts or if the dream would end.

## My Dark Angel

Dancing around her, worshiping her fire, protect-
    ing her soul, feeling her fire, as it burns out of
    control.
Troy M. Harmon. Thank you.

# ABOUT THE AUTHOR

Troy Harmon was born in St. Louis, Missouri. He goes to visit St. Louis every now and then. He grew up in southeast Missouri, along the Mississippi. Mostly they fished and hunted and had big bonfires and BBQs. Things were good back then when he was a young man, strong and ready to take on anything life threw at him till his family started to pass away one by one—his grandfather and grandmother. Then close friends passed to the other side, then aunts and uncles, then his mom, and shortly after his stepdad. They were together for forty years. Now it's just his brothers and sisters who are all that is left of the family. So now that he is getting older too, he thinks when he passes over to the other side, he'll take a walk through the universe. He thinks he'll take a walk in the skies.

9 798892 219075